BrAiN BENDERS

THINK OUTSIDE THE BOX

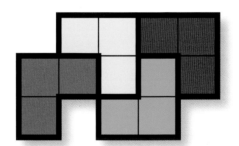

by Dr. Gareth Moore

HUNGRY TOMATO™

Contents

Think Outside the Box

Get ready to engage your brain and challenge your mind with a huge range of puzzles and games! To make it through the book you'll need to 'think outside the box' and really take advantage of your imagination!

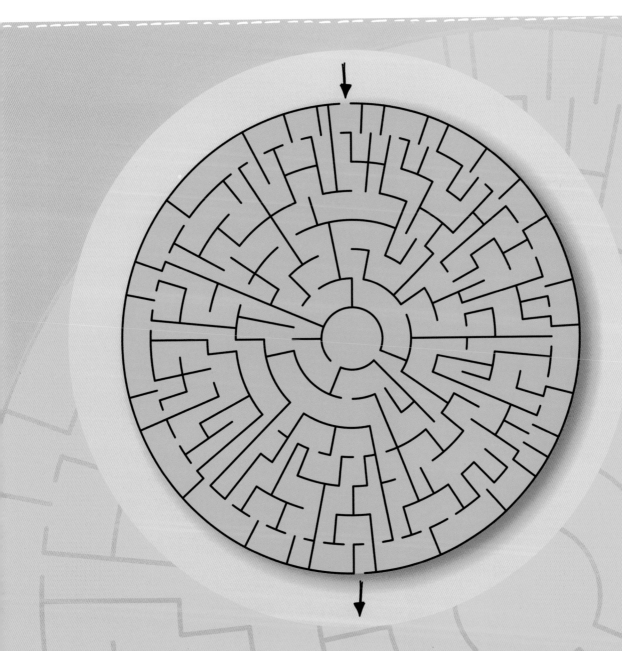

Here is an ingenious maze to start you off. Don't draw on the maze - that would be too easy. Solve it in your head.

Need help with solving this puzzle? Turn to pages 28 for helpful tips.

Seeing it in Your Head

You might not be able to move things around the room with just the power of your mind, but you can still imagine what it would look like if they did move! Let's test out the power of your imagination.

1 Sliding around

Look at these six tiles. Imagine sliding them around to new positions. What letter can you make?

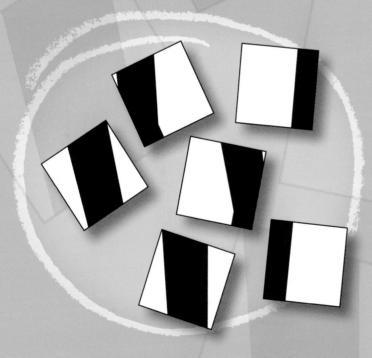

Now try these six tiles. What letter can you make if you put them back together?

2 Shape combination

Let's try to combine pictures with the power of your mind. If you remove the white squares from one picture and put it on top of the other, how many stars can you count?

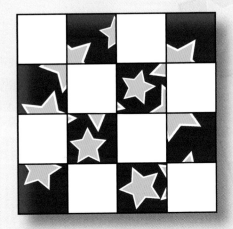

3 Stacking things up

Imagine you have four coloured tiles, A, B, C and D, as shown here, and each is printed on a piece of transparent plastic. What order would you stack them in to make each of the three pictures below, numbered 1, 2 and 3?

For example, if you put down D and then put C on top, you'll end up with a yellow oval on top of a blue rectangle.

A 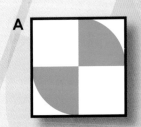 B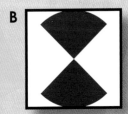

C 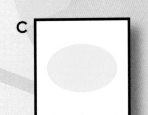 D

1    2    3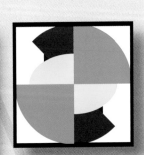

Need help with solving this puzzle? Turn to pages 26 to 29 for helpful tips.

Shape Fitting

Have you ever built a model, either from a kit or using your imagination?
How good are you at putting things together just in your head?

1 Cutting it up

This pattern has been cut up into **four** identical
pieces. Some of them have been rotated, but
they're all the same shape.

Can you use your imagination to work out how to cut each
of the following patterns into **four** identical shapes, too?

1

2

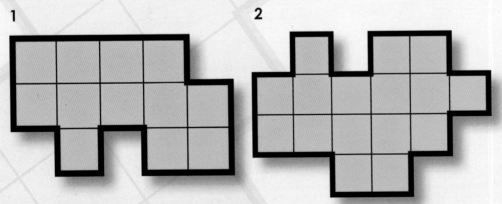

If you get
really stuck,
you could copy
them out and
use a pencil,
but try doing
them in your
head if
you can!

2 Cracking problem

Two of these pieces can be combined to make a whole egg, without any gaps. Can you work out which two?

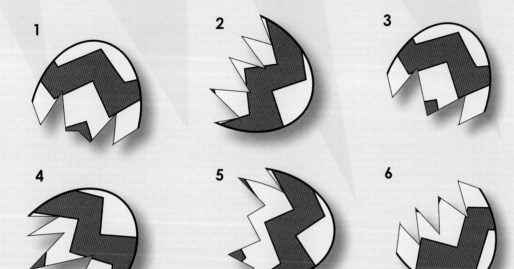

3 Access granted

Six different keys have each been pushed down into a piece of modelling clay to leave an imprint. Which of the numbered pieces of clay exactly matches the key shown here?

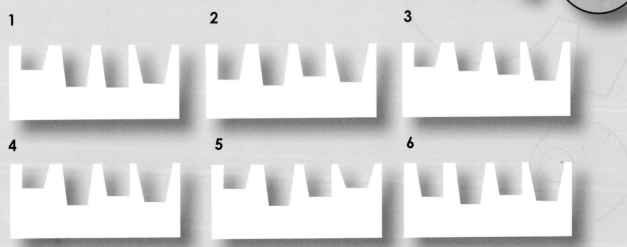

Need help with solving this puzzle? Turn to pages 26 to 29 for helpful tips.

Games for One

Have you ever played a pen and paper game with a friend, like noughts and crosses or battleships? Try these solo versions for just one player – no friend required! You'll still need the pen and paper.

1 Solo noughts and crosses

In two-player noughts and crosses, the aim is to get three Xs or three Os in a line. Here the aim is to fill the grid in such a way that you **never** get **four** Xs or Os in a line. Just like the two-player game, lines can run in any direction, including diagonally. Start by copying out every grid exactly as shown here.

To play it you need to write an O or X in every empty box without creating any lines of four. Try to do this by thinking about it, not just guessing! Unlike the two-player game, you don't need to alternate writing Os and Xs, so you might have more of one symbol than the other in the finished puzzle.

2 Solo battleships

Two-player battleships involves locating the other player's fleet of ships on the grid. This one-player version is just the same, but this time you are given some clues about where the ships are. You also no longer need to guess! The numbers at the end of each row and column tell you how many squares in that row or column contain part of a ship. There's also another rule that you might already know: two ships can't touch each other, not even diagonally.

Here's an example of a completed puzzle, where all of the ships have been found.

Battleships Fleet

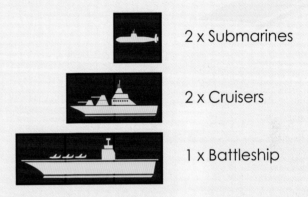

2 x Submarines

2 x Cruisers

1 x Battleship

Copy out each battleships grid, including the numbers next to it. Then try to find each of the listed ships on the grid. You can do this by thinking, not guessing.

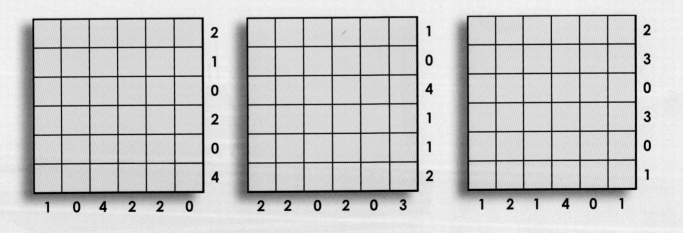

Need help with solving this puzzle? Turn to pages 26 to 29 for helpful tips.

11

An Unusual View

Do you notice the small details in the world around you, such as the pattern on a football player's shirt or the writing on the side of a pen or pencil? These pages are all about small details.

1 Close-up imagination

Have you ever made up a story? See what you can make up for each of these pictures. The artist has drawn something in close-up each time, but not told you what it is. What do you think the big picture might be?

For example, the first one could be the trunk and ear of an elephant lying on its back! What do **you** see when you look at these images?

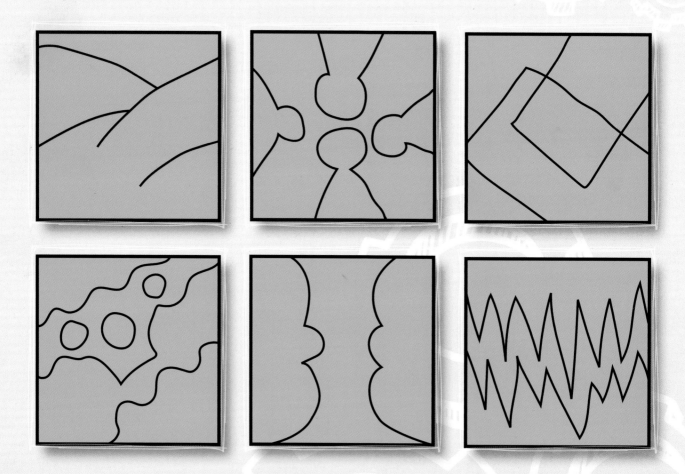

2 Close-up details

We've taken some close-up pictures of everyday objects.
You've probably seen or used all of these items before.

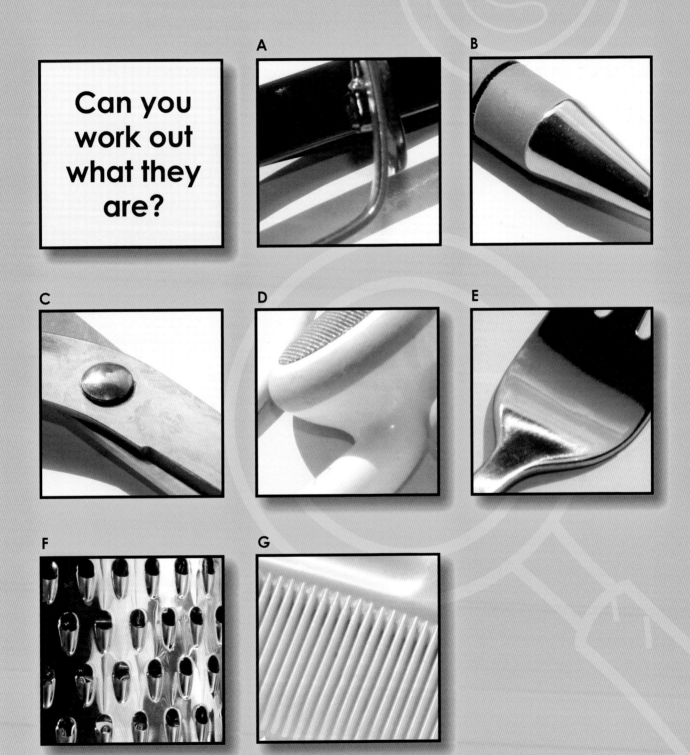

Can you work out what they are?

A

B

C

D

E

F

G

Need help with solving this puzzle? Turn to pages 26 to 29 for helpful tips.

Around and About

Have you ever tried reading a map or a plan of a building? It can sometimes be pretty confusing working out which way is left and right relative to where you're standing. These puzzles will help you practise those skills.

1 Rotated all round

Rotate each picture as shown by the arrow beneath it. So you rotate picture 1 by a quarter turn clockwise, 2 by a half turn and 3 by a quarter turn anticlockwise.

Which of the options below, A, B or C, would you end up with in each case?

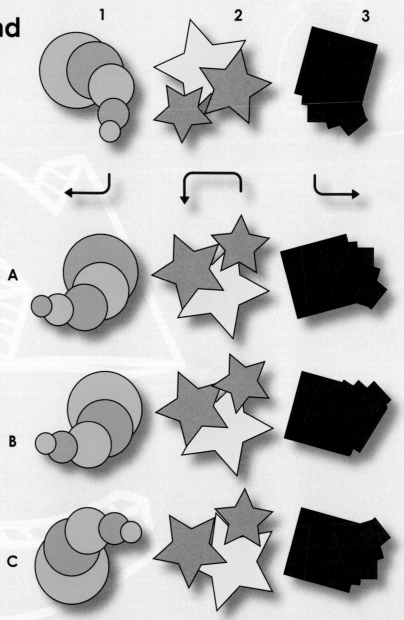

2 On reflection

If you look in a mirror and wave your right hand, in the reflection it looks like it's your left hand waving. Can you imagine what other things would look like if seen in a mirror?

Copy out these patterns onto a piece of paper, but in each case draw what you'd see if you held the book up in front of a mirror. Then fold your paper along the edge of your drawing and line it up against the edge of the pattern in the book. Have you drawn the reflection correctly? If you have, you'll reveal a simple picture!

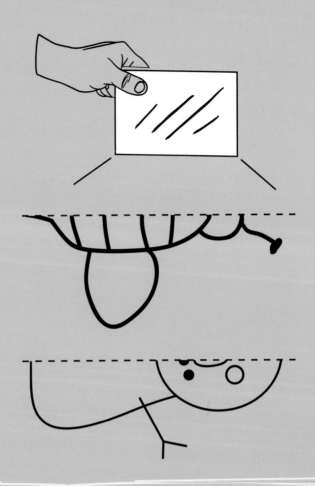

3 Mirror writing

Have you ever tried looking at your handwriting in a mirror? It can be pretty tricky to read! Can you work out what has been written here? If you get stuck, you could use a mirror to help you. See if you can write out your name so that it would appear the correct way around if you viewed it in a mirror. It's a lot trickier than it seems!

Next, try copying out these stick people so that they would look the same when reflected in a mirror. Use a mirror to see if you were correct!

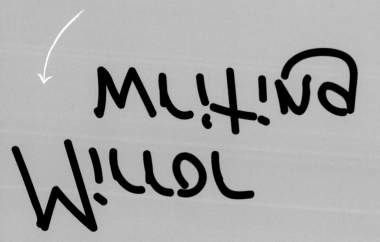

Need help with solving this puzzle? Turn to pages 26 to 29 for helpful tips.

15

3D Cubes

Have you ever tried drawing a picture of a three-dimensional object? You need to somehow represent the different distances you see with your eyes in a completely flat drawing on a piece of paper. It can be pretty tricky, but in these puzzles you'll do the opposite – you'll think about what some drawings would look like if they were real objects right in front of you.

1 Counting cubes

Look at this picture of some cubes. You can only directly see four cubes, but there must be a fifth there in order to stop the one on the top layer from falling down.

Now imagine that you start with an arrangement of cubes like the one in this picture. It is made up of 27 cubes, with 3 layers each with 9 cubes on.

Imagine that you now take away some of the cubes and end up with this picture. How many cubes are left in the arrangement?

And how many cubes are there in the arrangement on the far right?

Now imagine that you have an arrangement of 64 cubes set up like this, with 16 cubes on each of 4 layers.

If you start from this arrangement each time, how many cubes are there in each of the following pictures?

2 Folding cubes

Imagine that you were to cut out each of these different patterns and fold along the lines. Most of them can be folded up to make a perfect cube, with a solid surface on all six sides, but there are three exceptions. Which are the three odd ones out?

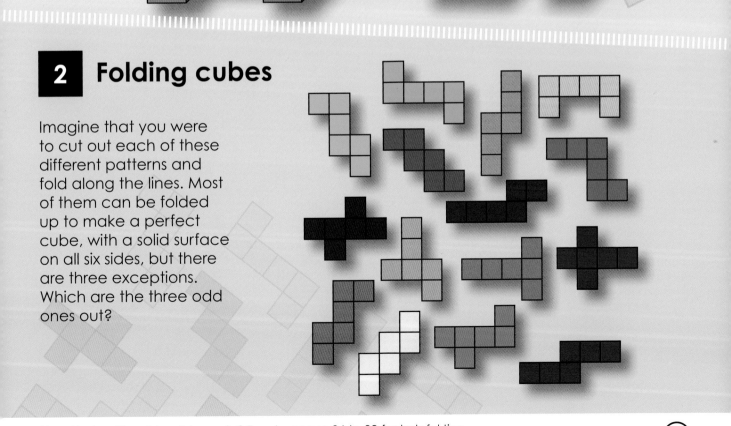

Need help with solving this puzzle? Turn to pages 26 to 29 for helpful tips.

Thinking in 3D

Do you have the power to build things entirely in your mind? These objects are all flat drawings but you can use your imagination to work out what they would look like if they were solid objects.

1 Odd cube out

Without actually trying it out, imagine that you had cut out each of these four patterns and then folded along the lines to make a cube. Three of them would be identical, but one would be different. Which one?

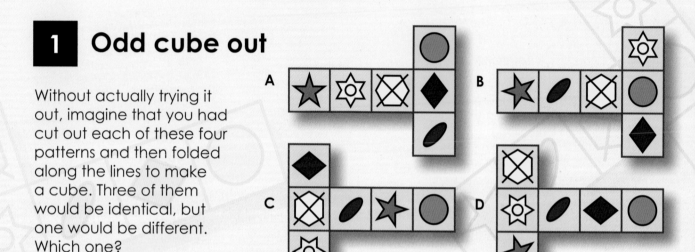

2 Pyramid power

The Ancient Egyptians built pyramids – and so can you, using just your brainpower! Imagine that each of these shape templates had been cut out and folded along the lines. Only two would make a four-sided pyramid without any missing sides – but which two?

3 Pop-up cubes

Have you ever tried drawing a picture of a cube where all the edges are visible, even those that are out of sight? This is called a wireframe cube.

With this red wireframe cube (below), do you see it as a cube that sits out to the front and left, as in the first blue picture, or as a cube that lifts up and to the right, as in the second blue picture? An X is marked on the front of each cube, to help you work the pictures out.

By looking at the red wireframe cube carefully, can you swap back and forth between both versions of the cube, and see it both ways? It can take some practice, but you can do it! You probably find the left-hand version easier to see, because you're more used to looking down on a cube object, such as a building block or a die, rather than looking up at it, as on the right. To see this view with a real cube you'd need to hold it above your eyes, or look up at it through a glass table.

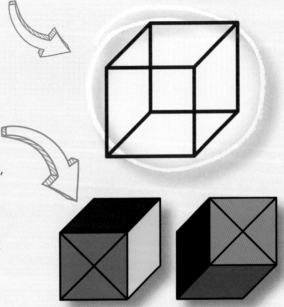

4 Even more pop-up cubes

Try these two wireframe cube pictures, too. In the left-hand one, can you see a cube that you are looking down on from above? Can you then also see a cube that you are looking up at from below? Both are there, but it might take you a bit longer to see the one from below. Keep trying – it can be quite an amazing effect when it suddenly 'pops up' in front of you!

If you managed that, try the second wireframe on the right. You can also see this as both a cube from above or a cube from below. And what's amazing is that this is just a regular hexagon with lines joining all of the opposite corners. Try drawing this out – it isn't obvious that this simple picture conceals two hidden cubes!

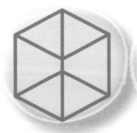

Need help with solving this puzzle? Turn to pages 26 to 29 for helpful tips.

Confusing Lines

You'll need to concentrate to solve the fiendish maze on this page.
Solve it in your head – don't draw on the maze. That would be too easy!

1 Circular maze

Can you find your way through this circular maze? Enter at the top and then make your way all the way through until you come out the bottom. Be careful, because the twisting circular shapes can make it easy to get stuck!

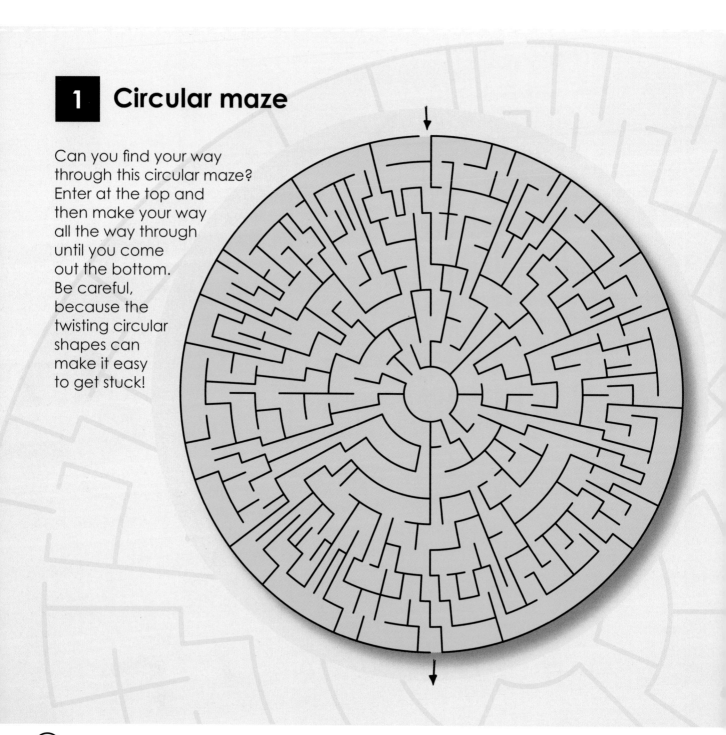

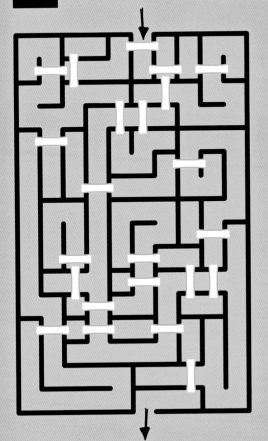

Have you ever been to a real-life maze where there are bridges you can use to cross over the paths? The mazes on this page are just like that, with bridges where one path crosses over another. Don't forget that you can go underneath them, too!

If you get stuck, retrace your steps and make sure that there isn't a route over or under a bridge that you missed.

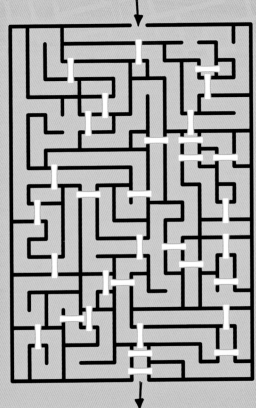

3 **Hidden star**

Can you find this star shape in this maze of lines? It may appear at a different rotation and size, but it will otherwise look exactly the same. You might find this surprisingly tricky!

Need help with solving this puzzle? Turn to pages 26 to 29 for helpful tips.

21

Hidden in Plain Sight

Military vehicles and soldiers wear camouflage to make them hard to spot in the heat of battle, and many animals are coloured or patterned to help them blend into their natural environments. Can you find all of the carefully hidden objects on these pages?

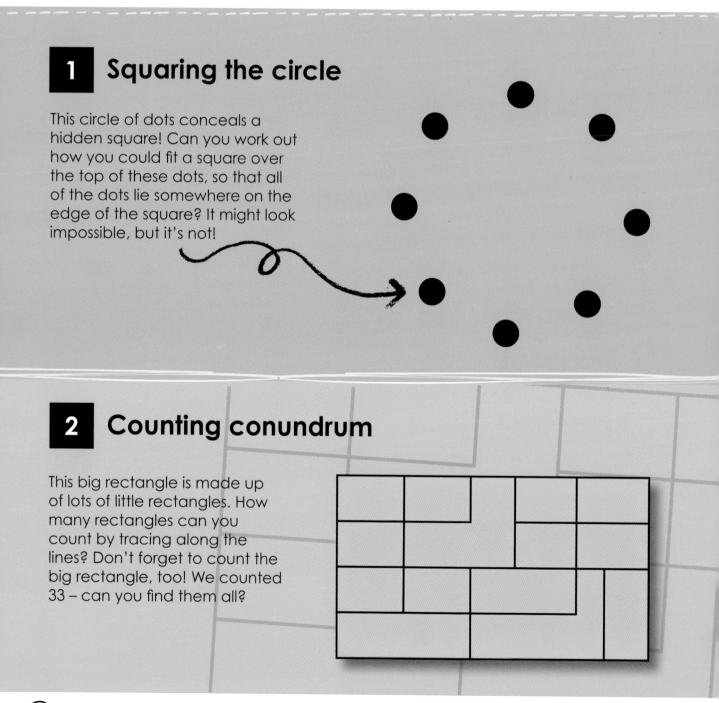

1 Squaring the circle

This circle of dots conceals a hidden square! Can you work out how you could fit a square over the top of these dots, so that all of the dots lie somewhere on the edge of the square? It might look impossible, but it's not!

2 Counting conundrum

This big rectangle is made up of lots of little rectangles. How many rectangles can you count by tracing along the lines? Don't forget to count the big rectangle, too! We counted 33 – can you find them all?

3 Secret writing

This might look like just a page of random typed letters, but try putting the book down and looking at it from a distance. What can you see now?

Need help with solving this puzzle? Turn to pages 26 to 29 for helpful tips.

Logic Challenges

It's amazing what you can do when you stop and think. All of the puzzles on these pages will be tricky if you try to solve them by guessing, but if you pause a moment and work things out, then you'll find they're a lot easier than they might seem!

1 Rows and columns

A square grid where exactly the same set of items appears once in every row and column is called a Latin square. Grids like this have been found dating back thousands of years, and sometimes were used just for decoration. The puzzles on this page all challenge you to fill a square grid with shapes to make a Latin square of your own.

Here are the four shapes to use

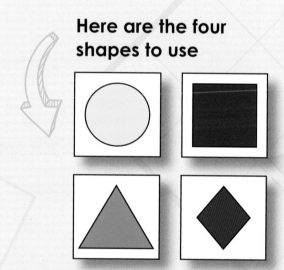

Start by copying out the first of these three grids onto a piece of paper. There's no need to colour in the shapes unless you want to. Once you've copied it, can you work out how to fill all of the empty squares so that each of the four shapes appears exactly once in every row and column? Then try the other two puzzles – each one is a little harder than the previous one.

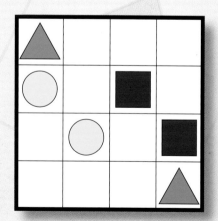
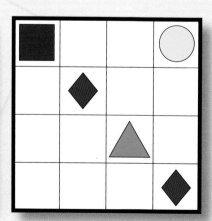

2 Extra regions, rows and columns

If you're familiar with Sudoku puzzles, you might recognize these next puzzles as being a bit like Sudoku, since the aim here is to also place one of each shape in each of the bold-lined regions. The finished grid still needs to form a Latin square, but now you must work with these extra regions, too. Start with the first puzzle and work up to the hardest one.

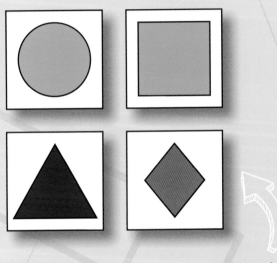

These are the four shapes to place in the grids. When you copy out the grids, there's again no need to copy the colours, unless you want to.

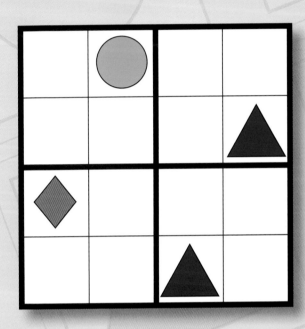

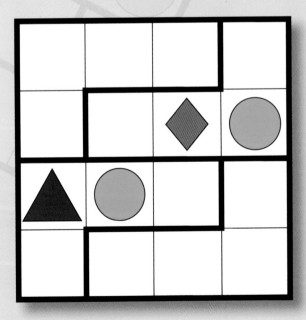

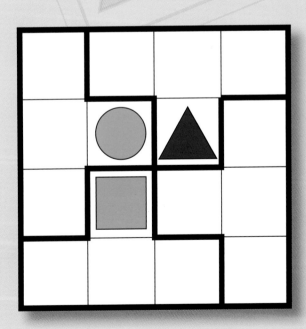

Need help with solving this puzzle? Turn to pages 26 to 29 for helpful tips.

Helpful Tips

Page 4
Introduction

See page 28 for hint.

Pages 6 – 7

Seeing it in Your Head

Sliding around

Instead of guessing, try using logic. Some of the pieces contain part of an image that continues off to the right, while others continue to the left, or up, or down. Use this information to start to imagine how they fit together. Think through each of the capital letters in the alphabet until you find one that fits.

Shape combination

Count the stars you see on one half of the puzzle, even if you can only see a bit of each one. Then, on the other half of the puzzle you need only add the whole stars that sit entirely within a square.

Stacking things up

Look for the colour that's at the back, and there's your first layer. Then find a colour that's on top of that one but beneath the other two, and there's your second layer, and so on.

Pages 8 – 9

Shape Fitting

Cutting it up

Start by counting the number of grid squares and then divide by four to work out how many squares are in each piece. Then you can look for bits of the pattern that stick out where you know two squares must go together. These will help you get going.

Cracking problem

Use a process of elimination. Pick any half and see if another half fits – if not then you can forget about the half you are looking at and move on.

Access granted

This puzzle is a Spot the Difference with six options. The spaces in the key will match the outline of one imprint. Compare each imprint in turn with the key until you find the exact fit.

Pages 10 – 11

Games For One

Solo noughts & crosses

You can solve these without guessing. Start by looking for any square which, if it contained an O, would make a line of four Os. If you find one, then it must have an X in it to avoid a line of four. Then check again for the opposite: squares that must have an O because an X would make a line.

Solo battleships

The key to this puzzle is to mark in not just the ships but also the 'misses': the squares you know must contain water. Start with the rows and columns marked 0 and put an X in every square to indicate 'miss'. Now are there any rows or columns where the number of ship segments equals the number of non-'miss' squares?

If so, you can shade all these in. Next, look at the list of ships you have to find. Is there only one place in the grid where one of these ships will fit? If so, mark it in! Don't forget to keep track of which ships you still need to find.

Pages 12 – 13

An Unusual View

Close-up imagination

There are no 'correct' answers here! You can always invent things if you can't think of anything real, so if you think it could be a monster from outer space then that's fine – to you, that's what it is!

Close-up details

If you get stuck, try asking a friend for help. Sometimes what's hidden to you can be obvious to someone else! Here are some clues to the objects:

- You use one of them in your hair.
- Two of them are kitchen implements.
- Two of them are stationery products.

- One of them you might put in your ears.
- One of them you might rest on your nose!

Pages 14 – 15

Around and About

Rotated all round

Look for the differences between the three options, and then think about which of these differences would be the correct one that matches the original.

On reflection

You might find it easier to copy these accurately if you start by tracing the start and end of the edges of each drawing onto a piece of paper. This will make sure you start at the same size and the result is more likely to line up.

Mirror writing

Try writing your name normally first and then look at it in a mirror and try copying it from there. Then cover that over and see if you can do it again without help! You can use a similar process with the stick people.

Pages 16 – 17

3D Cubes

Counting cubes

The secret is being organized by treating each layer in turn as a smaller, easier puzzle. Count all of the cubes in just the top layer and write down that number. Then repeat for each of the layers, add up all of the layer counts, and there's your overall answer! When counting, don't forget to include the 'hidden' cubes that you can't see. That's part of the challenge.

Folding cubes

One thing you can notice straight away is that some of the patterns are very similar. For example, any that are made up of four squares in a straight line

with one square sticking off to either side will definitely make a cube. You can imagine the four squares wrapping around in a loop,

and then the other two squares folding up as flaps to complete the cube.

If you start thinking about folding up each shape in this way, bit by bit, it can help. Another option, if you're really stuck, is to copy them out on paper, then carefully cut them out and fold them up – this can be quite fun to do anyway!

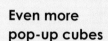

Pages 18 – 19

Thinking in 3D

Odd cube out

Each of the unfolded cubes has the same six shapes on it, so one method is to pick each of the six shapes in turn and think about how that shape would appear relative to each other shape on every cube. Consider both the shape's position on the cube and whether it has been rotated.

Pyramid power

You can eliminate the green option straight away because it only has three sides, not four. The others are trickier to think about, but you can make it easier by noticing that the yellow, blue and purple options are all exactly the same. Take a look at the orange one – can you imagine folding up the three edge triangles to form a pyramid?

Pop-up cubes

If you have trouble, try switching your vision back and forth between the wireframe and the solid blue cubes to help you focus on the parts of the image that will help you see the cubes in both orientations.

Even more pop-up cubes

Try drawing out solid versions of the cubes if you find this tricky. Then switch your vision back and forth between these and the wireframes. You could also pick up an actual cube, such as a building block or die, and compare with that.

Pages 5, 20 – 21

Confusing Lines

Circular mazes

You can't use a pen or pencil to draw on the maze, so the secret is to use your memory instead! Each time you reach a junction, try to remember the option you picked, so that if you go wrong you can avoid repeating the same mistake next time around!

Bridge mazes

Try to keep track in your head of which way you went at each junction! The path can travel over and under itself, so you can't assume that you need to move in the direction of the exit at all times – sometimes the correct route may appear to be going in the wrong direction!

Hidden star

Remember that the star may be a different size, and perhaps rotated, relative to the yellow picture. If you're still stuck, try paying most attention to the left-hand side of the drawing.

Pages 22 – 23

Hidden in Plain Sight

Squaring the circle

You know that you are looking for a square, and you have 8 dots. You also know that squares always have 4 straight sides, which means that at least four pairs of the dots must be linked by straight lines. Try imagining it as a dot-to-dot puzzle with the four corner dots all missing!

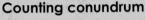

Counting conundrum

Invent a method to organize your counting, otherwise it's easy to miss out a rectangle or count one more than once. Consider each corner in turn, from left to right and top to bottom, and then count the number of rectangles that use each corner. Each rectangle has four corners so if you do this for every corner in the picture you'll end up counting each rectangle four times, so you'll need to divide your total count by four.

Another method is to make sure you only count each rectangle once, so for each corner in the picture you should only count the rectangles for which that corner is at the top-left corner of the rectangle. This will make sure you only count each rectangle once, since of course each rectangle only has one top-left corner!

Secret writing

If you can't see it, make sure you've put the book down, then go as far away as you can and look back. Can you see it now? It's an animal's face.

Pages 24 – 25

Logic Challenges

Rows and columns

Consider each row and column in turn – what shapes are missing? For each missing shape, see which empty squares it can fit in without repeating the shape in a row or column. If there's only one fit, place it! Another option is to pick an empty square and work through the shapes that might fit in it – if there's only one possibility, mark it in!

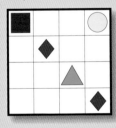

Extra regions, rows and columns

Use the tips for 'Rows and columns' on the left, but also check the regions. Look in each region to see what shapes are still missing, and if there's only one place you can fit a particular shape, mark it in!

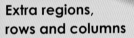

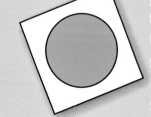

Answers

Page 5 Introduction

Pages 6 – 7 Seeing it in Your Head

Sliding around

Stacking things up

1) BDCA   2) ACDB   3) DBCA

Shape combination

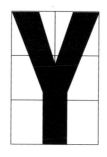

There are 15 stars

Pages 8 – 9

Shape Fitting

Cutting it up

Cracking problem

Pieces 2 and 6

Access granted

Imprint 4

Pages 10 – 11

Games For One

Solo noughts and crosses

Solo battleships

Page 13

An Unusual View

Close-up details

A) Pair of glasses

B) Pen

C) Scissors

D) Earphones

E) Fork

F) Grater

G) Comb

Pages 14 – 15 Around and About

Rotated all round

1) B

2) A

3) C

Mirror writing

The text says 'Mirror writing'.

On reflection

Pages 16 – 17 3D Cubes

Counting cubes

a) 16 cubes: 4 on layer 1, 5 on layer 2, 7 on layer 3

b) 11 cubes: 2 on layer 1, 2 on layer 2, 7 on layer 3

c) 33 cubes: 4 on layer 1, 6 on layer 2, 9 on layer 3, 14 on layer 4

d) 23 cubes: 1 on layer 1, 4 on layer 2, 6 on layer 3, 12 on layer 4

Folding cubes

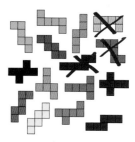

Thinking in 3D

Odd cube out

Shape net C is different – the pink ellipse is rotated compared to the other cubes.

Pyramid power

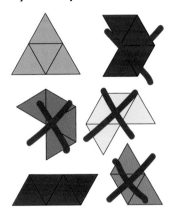

Confusing Lines

Circular maze

Hidden star

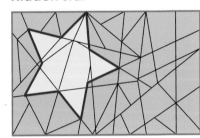

Bridge mazes

Hidden in Plain Sight

Squaring the circle

Counting conundrum

Counting the larger rectangles as well as smaller ones within them, you should get a total of 33.

Secret writing

Logic Challenges

Rows and columns

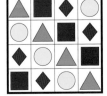 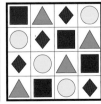 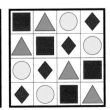

Extra regions, rows and columns

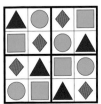 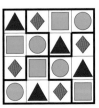

Index

About the Author

Dr. Gareth Moore is the author of a wide range of puzzle and brain-training books for both children and adults, including The Kids' Book of Puzzles, The Mammoth Book of Brain Games and The Rough Guide Book of Brain Training. He is also the founder of daily brain training site **www.BrainedUp.com**. He gained his Ph.D from Cambridge University (UK) in the field of computer speech recognition, teaching machines to understand spoken words.